SPECTRUM®
READERS

LEVEL 3

SPECTACULAR!
Caves

By Teresa Domnauer

Carson-Dellosa
Publishing

An imprint of Carson-Dellosa Publishing, LLC
P.O. Box 35665
Greensboro, NC 27425-5665

carsondellosa.com

Printed in the USA. All rights reserved.
ISBN 978-1-4838-0131-5

01-002141120

Caves are unique underground environments.
They can form in rock, water, and ice.
A hidden fairy world of crystal formations can be found inside some caves.
Animals are found in caves, too.
People from ancient cultures lived in caves.
Many caves remain unexplored, but scientists and adventurers are taking on the challenge of discovering their secrets.

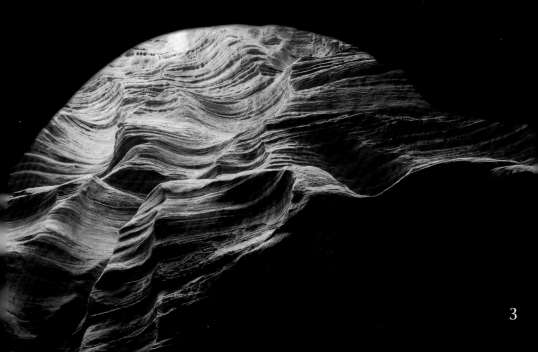

How Caves Form

It takes hundreds of thousands of years for caves to form.

First, rainwater soaks into the soil and then into cracks in the rock layer below. A chemical reaction happens between the water and soft rock such as limestone. Slowly, the water dissolves the rock. As the rock dissolves, hollow spaces, or caves, form underground.

Fascinating Facts

- Limestone is made from shells and skeletons of ancient sea creatures.
- Mammoth Caves in Kentucky is the world's longest cave system, with caves and tunnels over 300 miles long!

Inside a Cave

Inside most caves, it is dark and wet. Water drips from the ceiling, and pools form on the floor.

Fungi such as mushrooms and mold, which don't need light to grow, flourish. Colorful patterns formed by the mineral calcite often cover the walls.

These wall patterns are called *flowstones*.

Fascinating Facts

- Caves stay about the same temperature, even when the weather is very hot or cold above ground.

- The world's largest cave passage was discovered in Vietnam in 2009. Scientists walked nearly three miles inside before they ran into an obstacle.

Cave Formations

As water drips down from the roof of a cave, it collects minerals from the rocks. The mineral-filled water droplets form cones that hang from the ceiling of the cave like icicles.

These cones are called *stalactites*.

As water continues to drip from the bottom of the stalactites, cones build up on the cave floor.

These cones are called *stalagmites*.

Fascinating Facts

- When a stalactite and a stalagmite meet in the middle, they form a *column* like the one shown on page 16.

- Extremely thin stalactites are called *soda straws*.

Sea Caves

Caves also form along the ocean shore.
Crashing waves gradually wear away the
base of cliffs.
This creates an opening, or sea cave.
Oregon is home to one of the world's
largest sea cave systems, Sea Lion Caves.
Inside, Sea Lion Caves is as tall as a
twelve-story building!
Herds of sea lions live in and around
these caves.

Fascinating Facts

- Visitors to Sea Lion Caves take an elevator through 200 feet of solid rock.
- The Sea Lion Caves were formed over 25 million years ago.

Volcanic Caves

This cave in Spain, *Cueva de los Verdes,* is a volcanic cave.

These caves form when volcanoes erupt. Hot melted rock, or *lava,* flows down the side of a volcano.

The outer surface of the lava cools and hardens while hot liquid lava continues to flow inside.

Eventually, the lava drains out and leaves behind a *tube,* or tunnel-like cave.

Fascinating Facts

- *Cueva de los Verdes* formed when a volcano erupted over 3,000 years ago.
- The *Cueva de los Verdes* tunnel is nearly four miles long!

Ice Caves

Caves can form beneath glaciers.
Glaciers are slow-moving frozen rivers.
Water flowing underneath a glacier melts a
tunnel and forms a cave.
Other ice caves form when cold air reaches
underground caverns.
Moisture in the air freezes, creating huge
icicles, ice walls, and spectacular frozen
formations.

Fascinating Facts

- First explored in 1879, the world's largest
  ice cave can be found in the Alps near
  Salzburg, Austria.

- The inside of an ice cave appears blue
  when sunlight shines through the ice.

Carlsbad Caverns

Carlsbad Caverns is found in the Guadalupe Mountains of New Mexico. This national park has over 100 caves extending for 30 miles in a maze of underground rooms.

Visitors can use steps or an elevator to enter the Big Room at Carlsbad Caverns, one of the world's largest underground chambers.

Fascinating Facts

- Millions of years ago, an ancient sea covered the area of Carlsbad Caverns.
- Seventeen different bat species live at Carlsbad Caverns.

Slot Canyons

Slot canyons are caves with very deep, thin openings.

Colorful, striped rock formations are often found in slot canyons.

These canyons form when water rushes over sandstone for thousands of years.

Soft sandstone is easily eroded, or worn away, by water and wind.

Many of the world's slot canyons are found in the western United States.

Fascinating Facts

- The slot canyon at Buckskin Gulch in Utah is one of the longest in the world.

- Spooky Gulch slot canyon in Utah is so narrow that hikers must walk sideways to get through!

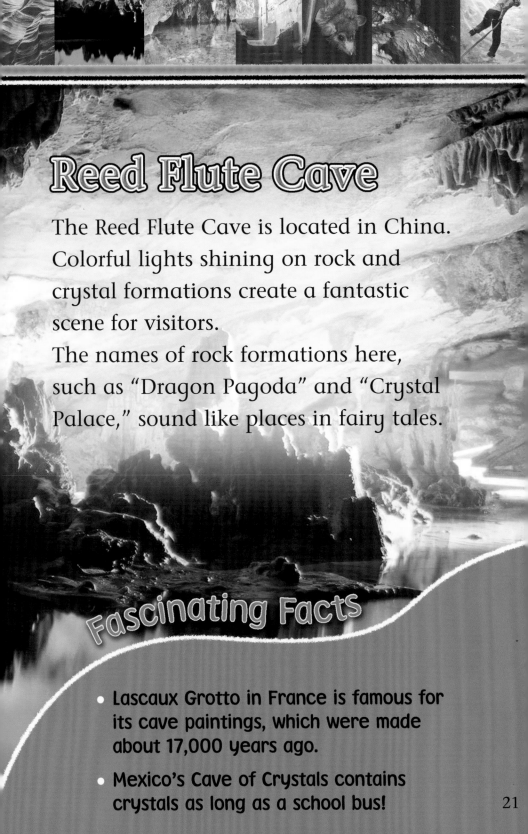

Reed Flute Cave

The Reed Flute Cave is located in China. Colorful lights shining on rock and crystal formations create a fantastic scene for visitors.

The names of rock formations here, such as "Dragon Pagoda" and "Crystal Palace," sound like places in fairy tales.

Fascinating Facts

- Lascaux Grotto in France is famous for its cave paintings, which were made about 17,000 years ago.

- Mexico's Cave of Crystals contains crystals as long as a school bus!

21

Cenotes

This sparkling pool of water surrounded by steep rock walls is a special kind of cave called a *cenote* (sih NO tee). These sinkholes form when the ceiling of a water-filled cavern collapses. They are found only in the Yucatán region of Mexico. Here, divers and snorkelers can explore miles of underground rivers connected to the cenotes.

Fascinating Facts

- In ancient times, cenotes were considered sacred because they were an important source of water.

- The word *cenote* means "well" in Spanish.

Cave Dwellings

About 700 years ago, the Salado people built homes inside these caves in Arizona. The cliff-side caves gave protection from sun, rain, and wind.

They also provided more living space, as many Salado villages on land were becoming crowded.

The caves were divided into 60 rooms. Today, the cave dwellings are part of the Tonto National Monument.

Fascinating Facts

- The first archaeologist visited the well-preserved cliff dwellings in 1883.
- The Salado people used ladders to climb up to different levels.

Cave Creatures

Many creatures live in caves, including insects, spiders, amphibians, and fish. Bats, especially, like to make their homes in quiet, protected caves.
Some caves contain hundreds of thousands of bats!
They sleep all day, hanging upside-down, in large groups called *colonies*.
When night falls, swarms of bats emerge to find food above ground.

Fascinating Facts

- This bat, the Egyptian fruit bat, roosts in caves in groups of thousands.
- Bats swat at each other with their wings to fight for the best roosting spots.

Spelunking

People who explore caves for sport and challenge are called *spelunkers*.

Spelunkers venture into dark, wet crevices and squeeze through tight spaces.

They carry rain gear, helmets, gloves, flashlights, and most importantly, spare batteries!

They must be prepared for dangers such as sinkholes or sudden flooding.

Fascinating Facts

- A spelunker never ventures into a cave alone. He or she always has a partner.

- If you've never been spelunking before, be sure to go with an experienced guide!

Studying Caves

Scientists who study caves are called *speleologists*.

For them, caves are underground labs. Studying caves can help determine when ice ages, droughts, and heavy rains occurred thousands of years ago.

This may help predict future weather patterns on Earth.

Fascinating Facts

- There are thousands of caves on our planet, but most of them are unexplored.

- The word *speleology* comes from the Greek words for "cave" and "study."

SPECTACULAR! Caves Comprehension Questions

1. What does a spelunker do?

2. Explain two ways that caves can form.

3. What is one reason that scientists study caves?

4. How long does it take for a cave to form?

5. What are stalactites?

6. What creatures live in caves?

7. Where is Carlsbad Caverns located?

8. What is the name for a scientist who studies caves?

9. How does water dissolve rock?

10. What is a flowstone?

11. Why is a volcanic cave called a *lava tube*?

12. What is a cenote?